SCHOLASTIC

writing guides

With interactive resources on CD-ROM

Life Stories

WITHDRAWN

for ages
9–11

Louise Carruthers
and Angel Scott

Credits

Authors
Louise Carruthers
and Angel Scott

Development Editors
Simret Brar and
Rachel Mackinnon

Editor
Liz Dalby

Assistant Editor
Alex Albrighton

Series Designer
Anna Oliwa

Designer
Paul Stockmans

Book Layout
Quadrum Solutions Ltd

Cover Illustration
Mark Oliver

Illustrations
Christopher Rothero
and Mike Phillips

CD-ROM Development
CD-ROM developed in
association with Infuze Ltd

Text © 2010 Louise Carruthers
Text © 2001, 2010 Angel Scott
© 2009 Scholastic Ltd

Designed using Adobe InDesign

Published by Scholastic Ltd,
Book End,
Range Road,
Witney,
Oxfordshire
OX29 0YD

www.scholastic.co.uk

Printed by Bell & Bain

1 2 3 4 5 6 7 8 9   0 1 2 3 4 5 6 7 8 9

British Library Cataloguing-in-Publication Data
A catalogue record for this book is available from the British Library.

ISBN 978-1407-11257-2

The rights of Louise Carruthers and Angel Scott to be identified as the authors of this work have been asserted by them in accordance with the Copyright, Designs and Patents Act 1988.
    Extracts from the Primary National Strategy's Primary Framework for Literacy (2006) www.standards.dfes.gov.uk/primaryframework © Crown copyright Reproduced under the terms of the Click Use Licence.

Acknowledgments
The publishers gratefully acknowledge permission to reproduce the following copyright material: **David Higham Associates** for the use of an extract from *Boy: Tales of Childhood* by Roald Dahl © 1984, Roald Dahl (1984, Puffin).
Hodder and Stoughton for the use of an extract from *Counting Stars* by David Almond © 2000, David Almond (2000, Hodder & Stoughton). Every effort has been made to trace copyright holders for the works reproduced in this book, and the publishers apologise for any inadvertent omissions.

CD-ROM Minimum specifications:
Windows 2000/XP/Vista   Mac OSX 10.4
Processor: 1 GHz   RAM: 512 MB   Graphics card: 32bit
Audio card: Yes   CD-ROM drive speed: 8x   Hard disk space: 200MB
Screen resolution: 800x600

Contents

Introduction: Life Stories

The *Writing Guides* series aims to inspire and motivate children as writers by using creative approaches. Each *Writing Guide* contains activities and photocopiable resources designed to develop children's understanding of a particular genre (for example, fairy stories). The activities are in line with the requirements of the National Curriculum and the recommendations in the *Primary Framework for Literacy*. The teacher resource books are accompanied by a CD-ROM containing a range of interactive activities and resources.

What's in the book?

The *Writing Guides* series provides a structured approach to developing children's writing. Each book is divided into four sections.

Section 1: Using good examples
Three text extracts are provided to explore the typical features of the genre.

Section 2: Developing writing
There are ten short, focussed writing tasks in this section. These are designed to develop children's ability to use the key features of the genre in their own writing. The teacher's notes explain the objective of each activity and provide guidance on delivery, including how to use the photocopiable pages and the materials on the CD-ROM.

Section 3: Writing
The three writing projects in this section require the children to produce an extended piece of writing using the key features of the genre.

Section 4: Review
This section consists of a 'Self review', 'Peer review' and 'Teacher review'. These can be used to evaluate how effectively the children have met the writing criteria for the genre.

What's on the CD-ROM?

The accompanying CD-ROM contains a range of motivating activities and resources. The activities can be used for independent work or can be used on an interactive whiteboard to enhance group teaching.
Each CD-ROM contains:
- three text extracts that illustrate the typical features of the genre
- interactive versions of selected photocopiable pages
- four photographs and an audio file to create imaginative contexts for writing
- a selection of writing templates and images which can be used to produce extended pieces of writing.

The interactive activities on the CD-ROM promote active learning and support a range of teaching approaches and learning styles. For example, drag and drop and sequencing activities will support kinaesthic learners.

Talk for writing

Each *Writing Guide* uses the principles of 'Talk for writing' to support children's writing development by providing opportunities for them to rehearse ideas orally in preparation for writing. 'Talk for writing' is promoted using a variety of teaching strategies including discussions, questioning and drama activities (such as, developing imaginative dialogue – see *Fantasy Stories for Ages 9–11*).

How to use the CD-ROM

Start screen: click on the 'Start' button to go to the main menu.

This section contains brief instructions on how to use the CD-ROM. For more detailed guidance, go to 'How to use the CD-ROM' on the start screen or click on the 'Help' button located in the top right-hand corner of the screen.

Installing the CD-ROM

Follow the instructions on the disk to install the CD-ROM onto your computer. Once the CD-ROM is installed, navigate to the program location and double click on the program icon to open it.

Main menu screen

Main menu

The main menu provides links to all of the writing activities and resources on the CD-ROM. Clicking on a button from the main menu will take you to a sub-menu that lists all of the activities and resources in that section. From here you have the option to 'Launch' the interactive activities, which may contain more than one screen, or print out the activities for pupils to complete by hand.

If you wish to return to a previous menu, click the 'Menu' button in the top right-hand corner of the screen; this acts as a 'back' button.

Screen tools

A range of simple writing tools that can be used in all of the writing activities are contained in the toolbar at the bottom of the screen.

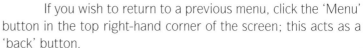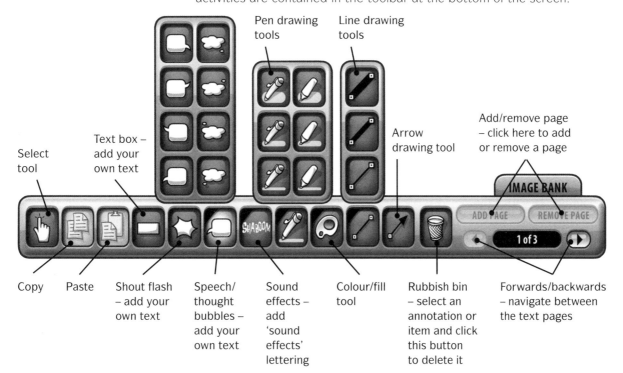

How to use the CD-ROM

Print

Save your work to chosen files

Open – navigate to your saved file to open your previous work

Reset the page

Printing and saving work

All of the resources on the CD-ROM are printable. You can also save and retrieve any annotations made on the writing activities. Click on the 'Controls' tab on the right-hand side of the screen to access the 'Print', 'Open', 'Save' and 'Reset screen' buttons.

View all thumbnails by clicking on the arrows

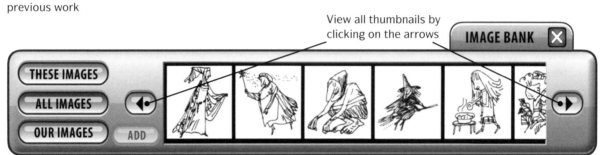

Image bank – click and drag an image to add it to an activity

Image bank

Each CD-ROM has an 'Image bank' containing images appropriate to the genre being taught. Click on the tab at the bottom right of the screen to open the 'Image bank'. On the left-hand side there are three large buttons.

- The 'These images' button will display only the images associated with the specific activity currently open.
- The 'All images' button will display all the photographs and illustrations available on the CD-ROM.
- The 'Our images' button will contain any images you or the children have added to the CD-ROM.

Press the left or right arrows to scroll through the images available. Select an image and drag and drop it into the desired location on the screen. If necessary, resize the image using the arrow icon that appears at the bottom right of the image.

You can upload images to the 'Image bank', including digital photographs or images drawn and scanned into the computer. Click on 'Our images' and then 'Add' to navigate to where the image is stored. A thumbnail picture will be added to the gallery.

Writing your own story

Each CD-ROM contains a selection of blank writing templates. The fiction genre templates will be categorised under the button 'My story' and the non-fiction templates will be categorised under 'My recount' or 'My writing'. The writing templates encourage the children to produce an extended piece of genre writing. They can also add images, speech bubbles and use other tools to enhance their work.

The fiction titles also include a cover template for the children to use. They can customise their cover by adding their own title, blurb and images.

Section 1
Using good examples

Life stories

A life story is an account of a person's life that can be written by the person themselves (autobiography) or by another person (biography). Life stories are a form of recount and so share many of the generic text structure and language features of recounted texts.

Exploring the genre

Through exploration of the extracts in the book and on the CD-ROM, the children will be introduced to some of the typical structural, organisational and language features of life stories. In addition to the extracts in the book and on the CD-ROM, you should provide opportunities for the children to read and explore other life stories. These could include:

- Life stories that detail a particular period or event in history, for example *The Diary of a Young Girl* by Anne Frank.

- Autobiographical poems, such as 'No breathing in class' by Michael Rosen

- Audio and audiovisual life stories, such as television documentaries.

Compare and contrast the life stories: distinguish between biography and autobiography; identify and analyse typical forms and features and recognise how these can be adapted to suit audience and purpose; explore the differences between fact and opinion, and implicit and explicit points of view; and encourage the children to infer the writers' viewpoint using not only what is written, but what is implied.

Links to the Primary Framework

In Years 5 and 6 there are a number of opportunities to develop children's understanding of and ability to use the features of biographical and autobiographical writing. These include:

- Year 5 Non-fiction Unit 2 'Recounts'

- Year 6 Non-fiction Unit 1 'Biography and autobiography' and Non-fiction Unit 4 'Formal/impersonal writing'

- Year 6 Additional text-based units 'There's a Boy in the Girls' Bathroom' and 'Street Child'.

Life story features

Structure
- Information is organised into paragraphs, sections or chapters with an appropriate opening and closing.
- Details are given to engage the reader.
- Content is organised chronologically.

Language features
- Written in the past tense.
- Written in the first or third person.
- Connectives are used to give order and structure to writing.

Form
- Life-story texts include: letters, diaries, autobiography, biography, news reports, weblogs, emails, obituaries and encyclopedic entries.

Section 1: Using good examples

Extract 1: Boy

What's on the CD-ROM

Boy
- An autobiographical account to read and discuss.

A special person in my life
- Choose a category.
- Describe a special person.

This extract demonstrates that autobiographical writing is a personal recount of events written to inform and entertain the reader.

- Read the extract together and define unfamiliar vocabulary. Identify the genre. Explore how Dahl has recounted his memories of the sweet-shop as though 'telling the story' of what happened.

- Ask the children to infer the significance of the sweet-shop in Dahl's life, highlighting evidence in the text to support their views. Talk about the 'centres' of other people's lives and what makes these places special.

- Hand out photocopiable pages 10 and 13 and ask the children to investigate how Dahl uses language to create an image of Mrs Pratchett and the sort of person she is. Discuss their responses. Do the children think Dahl has described the sweet-shop owner accurately? Why might he have exaggerated her characteristics?

- Talk to the children about people who have had an impact on their lives. Using the planning frame 'A special person in my life' on the CD-ROM (or photocopiable page 14) instruct the children to select one of the categories, make notes about a special person in their life and then use the notes to write a short character profile focusing on the details that make him/her special.

Extract 2: Easter chicks

What's on the CD-ROM

Easter chicks
- An autobiographical account to read and discuss.

A memorable moment
- Type notes to describe a memorable event.
- Type a full account of the event.

This extract exemplifies how description and detail can bring a life story alive for the reader.

- Read the extract with the children. Explain that this is one of a collection of stories the author has written about his childhood. Ask the children to consider why he has chosen to write about an event that he describes as 'a tiny incident, something that's almost nothing'. Why was the incident so memorable/significant in his life?

- Contrast Almond's grandad with Mrs Pratchett. Encourage the children to imagine what Mrs Pratchett would say about the chicks.

- Explore how detail and descriptive language bring the incident alive for the reader. Highlight the use of sense descriptions by asking the children to underline what Almond saw, heard, felt and smelled at different points on his journey.

- Ask the children to recount an experience that has left a lasting impression on them to a partner – for example, one that was amusing, scary or moving. Encourage them to describe in detail what happened, what they could see and hear, and how they felt.

- Ask the children to plan and write about an event in their life that has left a lasting impression on them using the CD-ROM activity 'A memorable moment' (or photocopiable page 15). Instruct them to write an account of the event as though telling the story of what happened (as in Extract 2).

Extract 3: Florence Nightingale

What's on the CD-ROM

Florence Nightingale
- An obituary to read, discuss and edit.

Autobiography and biography
- Roll over the headings to display the definitions.
- List the key features of each text type.

This extract can be used to investigate some of the key conventions of biographical writing.

- Read Extract 3 on the CD-ROM and discuss the purpose of an obituary. Draw attention to key structural, language and organisational features of this type of life story and highlight examples on the extract – for example, chronological sequence, introduction and concluding paragraph, connectives to link ideas and give structure to the writing, writing style and the use of complex sentences.

- Compare and contrast this life story with Extracts 1 and 2. Differentiate between autobiographical and biographical writing. Compile a list of the key features of each style of writing using 'Autobiography and biography' on the CD-ROM. Alternatively, you could ask the children to work in pairs using photocopiable page 16. Analyse the completed table to identify similarities and differences between the two types of writing. Circle the features on the chart that are common to both text types.

- Model rewriting a paragraph of Extract 3 as a piece of autobiographical writing using features listed in the table.

- Hand out photocopiable page 12 and ask the children to rewrite a different paragraph of text as autobiography. Encourage them to use their imagination to add personal details and description, and to give a subjective response to the events described.

Poster: Life stories

What's on the CD-ROM

Life stories
- Roll over the features on screens 1 and 2 to display the explanations.
- Read and discuss the poster information.

- Display the 'Life stories' poster from the CD-ROM. Explain that the poster summarises some of the generic features of life-story texts. Read and discuss the information contained in each section of the poster. Roll your mouse over each area to reveal additional information. (Please note, 'Written in the past tense' on screen 2 and all of screen 3 do not have roll over information.)

- Read and explore a range of life stories. Identify the main purpose (for example, to inform, to entertain), audience (for example, the public, a specific person or group of people) and features of each text type. Ask the children, in pairs, to record these details using an enlarged copy of photocopiable page 17 'Looking at life stories'.

- Display an enlarged copy of the 'Life stories' poster for the children to refer to throughout the course of a unit of work on life stories. Encourage the children to refer to the poster when planning and writing their own life stories.

Section 1: Using good examples

Extract 1: Boy

The sweet-shop was the very centre of our lives. Without it, there would have been little to live for. But it had one terrible drawback, this sweet-shop. The woman who owned it was a horror. We hated her and we had good reason for doing so.

Her name was Mrs Pratchett. She was a small skinny old hag with a mouth as sour as a green gooseberry. She never smiled. She never welcomed us when we went in, and the only times she spoke were when she said things like, "I'm watchin' you, so keep yer thievin' fingers off them chocolates!" Or "I don't want you in 'ere just to look around! Either you *forks* out or you *gets* out!"

But by far the most loathsome thing about Mrs Pratchett was the filth that clung around her. Her apron was grey and greasy. Her blouse had bits of breakfast all over it, toast-crumbs and tea stains and splotches of dried egg-yolk. It was her hands, however, that disturbed us most. They were disgusting. They were black with dirt and grime. They looked as though they had been putting lumps of coal on the fire all day long. And do not forget please that it was these very hands and fingers that she plunged into the sweet-jars when we asked for a pennyworth of Treacle Toffee or Wine Gums or Nut Clusters or whatever. The mere sight of her grimy right hand with its black fingernails digging an ounce of Chocolate Fudge out of a jar would have caused a starving tramp to go running from the shop. But not us. Sweets were our life-blood. We would have put up with far worse than that to get them. So we simply stood and watched in sullen silence while this disgusting old woman stirred around inside the jars with her foul fingers.

From *Boy, Tales of Childhood* by Roald Dahl

Text © 1984, Roald Dahl

Extract 2: Easter chicks

It was a tiny incident, something that's almost nothing, but it's stayed with me ever since it happened. It was mid-way through the school holidays, and I felt a great thrill of freedom as I walked out of the house alone, and out of the estate. I crossed Rectory Road, where the trees were in bright green leaf and grass was growing thickly on the verges, and entered the narrow lane to Windy Ridge, where the allotments were. The sun was shining. The greenhouses glittered. The air was filled with the scent of newly-turned earth and wood smoke.

I reached up and opened the gate. Grandad was sitting on the low brick wall of a cold frame. He wore his navy blue suit as always, his checked cloth cap as always, and was smoking his pipe as always. He turned to me as my feet crunched on the cinder path.

"Everybody all right?" he said.

"Aye."

"Howay, then. Something to show you."

Then he opened the door of the greenhouse: brilliant light and heat, and the sweet powdery scent of tomato plants. There was a cardboard box on a bench, a distant squeaking and scratching.

"Aye," he said. "In there."

I leaned closer and looked down into the box. There were a dozen chicks or more, tiny and bright yellow, shuffling together, squeaking together. I reached in and felt the sharp beaks and soft feathers, the delicate bodies trembling with new life. I lifted one from the box, cupped it in my hand, held it to my face. I laughed at the tiny claws scratching at my skin, at the tiny eyes, the tiny voice.

"Can this one be mine?"

"Aye. That one can be yours."

From *Counting Stars* by David Almond

Text © 2000, David Almond; illustrations © 2001, Christopher Rothero.

Section 1: Using good examples

Extract 3: Florence Nightingale

13 August 1910

Florence Nightingale, who has died aged 90, became famous at the time of the Crimean War for her work at the British military hospital in Scutari, Turkey. By the age of 35 she was a household name and she played a major role in making nursing a respectable profession for women.

Born in 1820 to wealthy parents, Florence grew up in a privileged atmosphere. She was educated at home with her sister and unlike most girls at that time studied a wide range of subjects. Nevertheless, Florence's parents still expected their daughter to marry and raise a family and they were shocked when Florence said she wanted to devote her life to nursing.

Eventually Florence overcame her family's opposition and in 1853 she was appointed superintendent of a hospital for sick gentlewomen in London. Later the same year, war broke out between Russia and Turkey in the Crimea and in 1854 Florence was asked to lead a team of nurses to the military hospitals in Turkey. This was her real opportunity to make a difference and her work in improving conditions for wounded soldiers made her famous as 'the Lady with the Lamp'.

Florence returned to England in 1856 and continued to work hard to improve nursing standards for many years, despite suffering from ill health. She set up the Nightingale Training School for Nurses in 1860 and wrote *Notes on Nursing*, which was translated into many languages.

Although Florence did not seek fame, her achievements were recognised during her lifetime and in 1907 she became the first woman to be awarded the Order of Merit by King Edward VII.

Illustrations © 2010, Mike Phillips/Beehive Illustration.

Mrs Pratchett

● Look again at the text. Write what Roald Dahl says about Mrs Pratchett's words, her clothes and her hands. Then write what it makes you think and feel as a reader.

	What is said in the text	How it makes me think and feel as a reader
What Mrs Pratchett says		
What Mrs Pratchett is wearing		
Mrs Pratchett's hands		

Illustrations © 2001, Christopher Rothero.

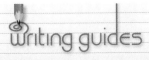

Section 1: Using good examples

A special person in my life

● Think of people who have been important in your life. What makes them special? Choose one of the categories below and make notes about your chosen person.

> Someone who helps me

> Someone who makes me laugh

> Someone I share an interest with

> Someone I look up to

> Someone I am close to

Name: _____

Appearance: _____

_____

Character: _____

_____

A memorable story: _____

_____

_____

Something they said to me:

Illustrations © 2010, Mike Phillips/Beehive Illustration.

A memorable moment

● Think of an incident in your past that has left a lasting impression on you. Make notes about what happened in the boxes below and then write about the event as though you are telling the story of what happened.

How old were you?	Where did the incident take place?
What could you see, hear and smell?	Who else was there?
What happened?	How did you feel?
Why will you always remember the event?	

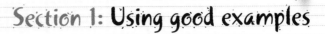

Photocopiable SCHOLASTIC
www.scholastic.co.uk

Autobiography and biography

- A life story is an account of a person's life that can be written by the person themselves (autobiography) or by another person (biography).
- Using the table below, compare and contrast the features of autobiographical and biographical writing.

Features of autobiographical life stories	Features of biographical life stories

Illustrations © 2010, Mike Phillips/Beehive Illustration.

Looking at life stories

• Read and investigate a range of life stories. Work with a partner to fill in the chart below.

Life story	Audience	Purpose	Biography/ autobiography	Features

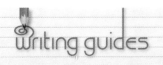

Section 1: Using good examples

Life stories

A life story is an account of a person's life that can be written by the person themselves (autobiography) or by another person (biography).

Text structure	Language features	Forms
• Content is organised into sections, for example, paragraphs/chapters covering different time periods or events.	• Written in the first (I, we) or third (he, she, they) person.	• Diary entry
	• Written in the past tense.	• Letter or email
• Each section has an opening (Who? What? Where? When?)	• Connectives link ideas within and between paragraphs – for example, some years later, however, as a result.	• Autobiography
• Details are recounted in chronological order. These may include facts, descriptive detail and personal reactions to events and experiences.		• Biography
		• News report
	• Writing style and vocabulary choices are appropriate to purpose and audience – for example, a diary entry is informal and subjective.	• Blog
• Each section is concluded appropriately for example, by summarising or reflecting on events.		• Obituary
		• CV

Section 2
Developing writing

Developing life story writing

The activities in this section aim to develop children's understanding of, and ability to use, some of the typical features of biographical and autobiographical writing in preparation for writing their own life-story texts. The activities provide meaningful contexts for writing, drawing on the children's own interests and experiences where appropriate.

Each of the activities focuses on developing a specific aspect of the genre. These include:

- Purpose: How form, style and purpose can be adapted to suit a particular audience and purpose. Children will be shown how to construct a piece of biographical writing based on research and be given opportunities to develop autobiographical writing in role.

- Text structure: Children will learn how to use a timeline to organise information chronologically and divide material into sections in preparation for writing a life story. The three-part structure of a life story (introduction, main events, ending) will be explored.

- Sentence/word level features: Children will be taught how to use temporal connectives to give order and structure to their writing and how to use subordinate clauses to add detail to complex sentences.

- Writers' knowledge: Through completing the activities in this section the children will develop awareness of the specific writers' knowledge required to write an effective life story including the selection of appropriate facts and details to bring events to life.

How to use the activities

A range of different teaching approaches are suggested to help children gain new skills and to stimulate ideas, which are then developed through whole-class, paired and individual work. The notes that accompany each activity give detailed instructions about how to deliver the activities, including how to use the photocopiable sheet and, where appropriate, how to use the interactive materials on the CD-ROM.

The suggested activities and teaching approaches are very specific but can easily be modified to take account of the specific needs, learning styles and interests of a particular group of learners.

Activity breakdown

Text structure
- This is my life (page 20)
- Life-story research (page 20)
- Timeline (page 21)
- Author biography (page 22)

Language features
- Obituary (page 21)
- Curriculum vitae (page 22)
- Medal winner (page 23)
- Writing for different audiences (page 23)
- Diary writing (page 24)
- Connectives (page 24)

Activity 1: This is my life

Objective

To use a range of oral techniques to present persuasive arguments and engaging narratives. (Year 6 Strand 1)

What's on the CD-ROM

Boy and Easter chicks
- Examples of autobiographical life stories.

What to do

In this activity, the children present an oral recount of significant events in their life so far.

- Read Extracts 1 and 2. Identify the text type (autobiography) and ask the children to recall some of the features of autobiographical writing. Highlight examples of these features on the texts. Recall the purpose of the text type (to entertain and inform) and explore how the authors have used a range of adjectives, adverbs, powerful verbs and phrases to achieve different effects.

- Explain that an autobiography is a 'selective account' of the writer's life. Making reference to Extracts 1 and 2, establish that the writers chose to write about people, places and events that have left a lasting impression. Compile a list of significant incidents in the children's lives to date that they might include in their own life stories.

- Hand out photocopiable page 25 'This is my life'. Ask the children to work independently and to make notes in each of the boxes, cut them out and arrange them in chronological order.

- Ask the children to use their notes to structure an oral recount of their life story to a partner. Remind them to include both factual information (who, what, where, when) and personal response (how they felt) relating to each event. Encourage them to use vocabulary effectively to engage the attention and interest of the listener.

Activity 2: Life-story research

Objective

To make notes on and use evidence from across a text to explain events or ideas. (Year 5 Strand 7)

What's on the CD-ROM

Florence Nightingale
- Example of an obituary of an historical person.

What to do

In this activity, children use a variety of biographical and autobiographical sources to research information about the life of a particular person.

- Choose a person the children have studied in another curriculum area to be the focus of research. Provide a collection of biographical sources of information about the person. Explore the material using key skills, such as skimming, to identify key dates and events in their life.

- Appraise each of the information sources. Identify the main purpose, audience and viewpoint. Consider the potential for author bias and how this may influence the reader's view of events.

- Ask the children to use photocopiable page 26 'Life-story research' to record information about significant events in the person's life.

- Now explore autobiographical accounts of the same person's life. Consider how the information contained in the autobiographical sources differs from that contained in the biographical accounts. Ask: *What other information do they give? Why?* For example, a diary entry may give a more subjective account of events. Allow time for children to note down additional information.

Activity 3: Timeline

Objective

To experiment with the order of sections and paragraphs to achieve different effects.
(Year 5 Strand 10)

What's on the CD-ROM

Florence Nightingale
● Example of an obituary of an historical person.

Timeline
● Record key dates and information on a timeline.

What to do

In this activity, the children are shown how to divide information into clear paragraphs for writing by organising the facts onto a timeline.

● Using Extract 3 and other suitable texts, explore some of the main structural and language features of biographical texts. For example, chronological order, information divided into clear sections.

● Explain that you would like the children to plan how to organise the information they collected in a previous activity into a piece of biographical writing. Open 'Timeline' from the CD-ROM and model how to use the information collected in Activity 2 to create a timeline of the major events in the person's life. Save the timeline for use in the next activity. (Alternatively, you could use copies of photocopiable page 27 'Timeline'.)

● Let the children create their own timeline using the information they recorded on photocopiable page 26 'Life-story research' in the previous lesson, and then split the timeline into sections to create suitable sections/paragraphs for writing.

● Ask the children to use their timelines to structure an oral recount to a partner using the key language features of life stories.

Activity 4: Obituary

Objective

To adapt sentence construction to different text types, purposes and readers. (Year 5 Strand 11)

What's on the CD-ROM

Florence Nightingale
● Example of an obituary of an historical person.

Timeline
● Open and review a timeline from a previous activity.

What to do

In this activity, the children use subordinate clauses to add detail to complex sentences.

● Begin by reading Extract 3 from the CD-ROM and other suitable examples of news obituaries. Identify the purpose (to give notice of a person's death and a short account of their life) and audience (the public) of this form of life story. Discuss the structure and organisation of the texts. Consider the formal writing style and contrast this with other life-story texts the children have studied.

● Open 'Timeline' from the CD-ROM and look at the saved file from the previous activity. In shared writing, model how to develop the information contained in the timeline into an obituary using the subdivisions on the timeline to organise information into appropriate paragraphs. Demonstrate how to construct sentences in a variety of ways and to how to use punctuation to clarify meaning.

● Hand out photocopiable page 28 'Complex sentences' and Extract 3. Revise the use of complex sentences and then ask the children to plan four complex sentences to include in an obituary about the person who was the subject of research in Activity 2.

● In a subsequent session, ask the children to write a complete obituary using the sentences they have recorded on the photocopiable sheet.

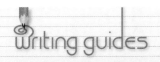

Activity 5: Author biography

Objective

To use varied structures to shape and organise text coherently.
(Year 6 Strand 10)

What's on the CD-ROM

Author biography
- Use the planning frame to make notes for an author biography.
- Roll over each heading to reveal further prompts.

What to do

In this activity, the children plan and write a short author biography.

- Read and investigate a selection of author biographies on different publishers' websites. Identify the main purpose of this type of life story. Explore what information is typically included in an author biography, how the information is organised and the style of writing.

- Using the activity 'Author biography' on the CD-ROM, make a shared plan for an author biography of a well-known author using the internet to research facts. In shared writing demonstrate how to expand the notes into a piece of biographical writing which includes a short opening paragraph introducing the author and summarising what they are best known for, and a closing statement.

- Organise the children in small groups to use the internet to research information about the life and work of a favourite author. Ask them to use 'Author biography' on the CD-ROM as a planning frame to make notes, or alternatively hand out photocopiable page 29 'Author biography' for them to use to plan ideas.

- Ask the children to write a short biography of their chosen author by turning the notes in each box into a paragraph with three to four sentences in it. Encourage the children to use a variety of simple and complex sentences, and to maintain an appropriate style throughout.

Activity 6: Curriculum vitae

Objective

To establish, balance and maintain viewpoints in non-narrative writing.
(Year 6 Strand 9)

What's on the CD-ROM

Curriculum vitae
- Roll over headings to view two job advertisements.
- Complete a fictional CV.

What to do

In this activity, the children will develop the skills of autobiographical writing in role by writing a CV.

- Show the class an example of a curriculum vitae (CV). Explain that a CV is a short summary of a person's education, qualifications and employment history which is often requested by an employer when someone is applying for a job.

- Discuss other examples of CVs, commenting on purpose, audience and form. Consider the style of writing (impersonal) and how this effect has been achieved, highlighting appropriate evidence on the text. Point out that a CV does not represent a person's complete life story, only experiences that are relevant to the job they are applying for.

- Open 'Curriculum vitae' on the CD-ROM roll over the headings of the job advertisements to reveal the text. In shared writing, complete the CV in role as a person applying for one of the jobs.

- Ask the children to write their own fictional CV for one of the jobs advertised on 'Curriculum vitae'. Encourage them to maintain an impersonal style by using vocabulary and sentence structures appropriate to the form and purpose of the writing. Alternatively, ask the children to complete photocopiable page 30 'Curriculum vitae'.

Activity 7: Medal winner

Objective

To make notes when listening for a sustained period and discuss how note-taking varies depending on content and purpose. (Year 6 Strand 2)

What's on the CD-ROM

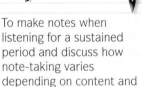

Media resources
- Listen to and discuss the audio clip.
- Use the 'Medal winner' image as a stimulus for discussion.

What to do

In this activity, children will listen to a person being interviewed about an important event in their life. They will use simple note-taking techniques to record the key information contained in the clip.

- Display the image 'Medal winner'. Talk about the image. Ask: *Where and when was the picture taken? Who is shown in the photograph? What is happening?* In small groups use hot-seating to explore what might have happened to the medal winner in the period of time before the photograph was taken. For example: *Which event did they compete in? How did they feel at the start of the race or competition? Did they set a new world record?* Allow each group to feed back ideas to the class.

- Tell the children that you are going to play an audio clip of the medal winner being interviewed after the medal ceremony. Ask the children to predict what questions the interviewer might ask before handing out enlarged copies of photocopiable page 31 'Medal winner' to provide a framework for note-taking. Remind children of simple note-taking techniques, such as selecting key words and using simple abbreviations. Play the clip several times and ask the children to make short notes under each heading.

- Encouraging children to refer to the notes they have taken, discuss the content of the audio clip. Ask the children to differentiate between facts and personal response. Instruct them to use two different colours identify factual information and subjective response on their notes.

Activity 8: Writing for different audiences

Objective

To select words and language drawing on their knowledge of literary features and formal and informal writing. (Year 6 Strand 9)

What's on the CD-ROM

Media resources
- Listen to the audio clip.
- Discuss the 'Medal winner' image.

News report
- Complete the template to create a newspaper report.

What to do

In this activity, children are shown how to write an account of the same life story for two different audiences.

- Look at the image 'Medal winner' and listen to the audio clip on the CD-ROM. Invite two volunteers to recount the medal winner's story to the group. Ask the first child to tell the life story in role as the athlete who has just received the medal, and the second child to recount what happened in the style of a news report.

- Compare and contrast the two accounts and compile a list of similarities and differences on the board.

- Demonstrate how to use the notes the children made in Activity 7 to write the opening paragraphs for two different life-story texts – a newspaper report and a letter to a close friend. Model how to use writing style and vocabulary appropriate to the form, purpose and audience of each example.

- Ask the children to continue one of the texts begun in shared writing. The children writing a newspaper report can use 'News report' on the CD-ROM or photocopiable page 32 as a writing frame.

Activity 9: Diary writing

Objective

To improvise using a range of drama strategies and conventions to explore themes such as hopes, fears and desires.
(Year 6 Strand 4)

What's on the CD-ROM

Media resources
- Use the 'Second World War evacuees' image as a stimulus for discussion.

What to do

In this activity, the children use hot-seating and role play to generate ideas for a simulated autobiography.

- Discuss what a diary is and explore children's experience of keeping diaries. Do any of the children keep a diary? What do they write in them? Do they let other people read their diary? Share with the children examples of published diary entries (for example, Anne Frank, Samuel Pepys) and, if appropriate, compare and contrast how writers from different times present experiences and use language.

- Discuss the purpose and audience of these life-story texts and highlight common features, such as date and time, informal writing style, details about events, people and places, personal/private.

- Display the image 'Second World War evacuees' from the CD-ROM and talk about what is happening. Ask: *Who are the children? What are they carrying? Where are they going? How are they feeling?* Explain that you would like the children to pretend they are one of the children. Use drama techniques including freeze-framing and thought-tracking to explore significant events, such as the evacuees saying goodbye to their families or their first sight of the countryside.

- Hand out copies of photocopiable page 33 'An evacuee's diary' and ask the children to continue the diary entry.

Activity 10: Connectives

Objective

To use varied structures to shape and organise text coherently.
(Year 6 Strand 10)

What's on the CD-ROM

Connectives
- Sort the connectives.

What to do

In this activity, children investigate how connectives are used to connect words and phrases.

- Discuss what the children know about connectives and how they can be used to give order and structure to writing. Organise the children to work in pairs or small groups. Give each group a life story such as a letter, an obituary or an extract from a biography or autobiography. Ask the children to underline the connectives.

- In feedback, compile a list of all the connectives the children have found. Talk about how different connectives have been used to achieve particular effects. For example, to indicate time (subsequently, first), opposition (but, however), addition (furthermore, also) and cause (so, therefore).

- Ask the children to complete the activity 'Connectives' on the CD-ROM or photocopiable page 34 by sorting the connectives into the correct columns in the table.

- Finally, ask the children to return to the piece of writing they produced in an earlier activity and to edit their work by adding connectives. You may wish to model this first, using a life story created in shared writing.

This is my life

● Think of people, places and events in your life so far that have made a lasting impression. Make notes about some of these experiences in the boxes below.

Greatest achievement	Oldest memory
Funniest memory	**Favourite place**
A special person	

Illustrations © 2010, Mike Phillips/Beehive Illustration.

● Cut out the boxes and arrange them in chronological order. Find a partner and tell them your life story.

Life-story research

● Use a range of biographical and autobiographical sources of information to investigate the life of a particular person. Make notes about key events in his/her life in the chart below.

Person's name _____

Year	Event	Details

Illustrations © 2010, Mike Phillips/Beehive Illustration.

writing guides

Timeline

• Organise the notes you made about the life of your chosen person onto the timeline below.

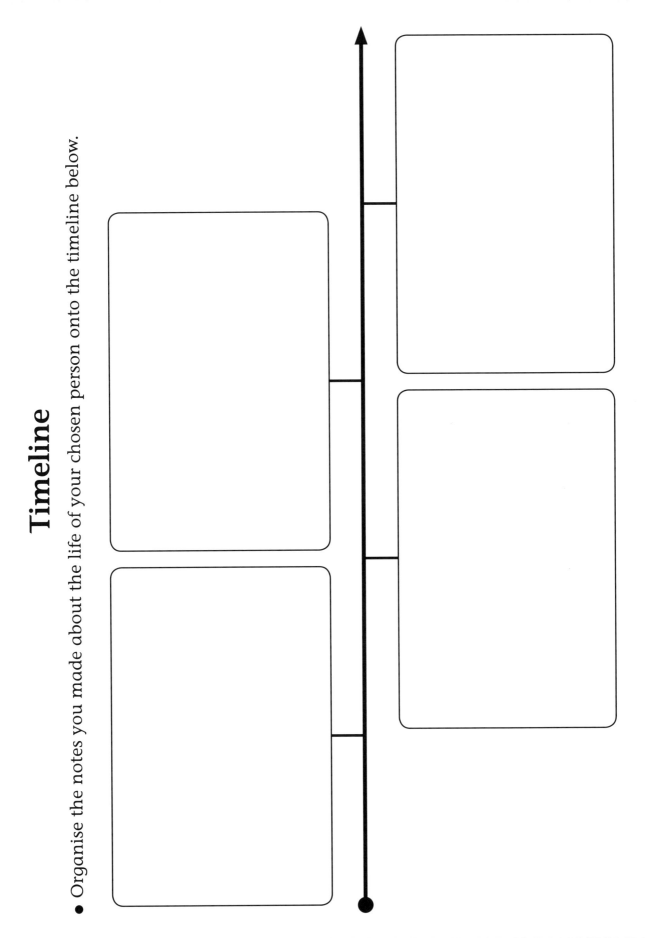

Photocopiable ◾SCHOLASTIC
www.scholastic.co.uk

Complex sentences

Complex sentences hold more than one piece of information. They contain a main clause (a complete short sentence) and a subordinate clause (that does not make sense on its own).

Commas are used to clarify the meaning when the subordinate clause comes at the beginning of the sentence or splits the main clause.

For example:

subordinate clause

Although she did not seek fame, Florence Nightingale's achievements were recognised during her lifetime.

subordinate clause

Florence Nightingale, who has died aged 90, became famous at the time of the Crimean War.

● Read Extract 3 and underline all of the complex sentences.
● Construct four complex sentences to use in an obituary of the person you have been researching.

1. _____

_____

2. _____

_____

3. _____

_____

4. _____

_____

writing guides

Author biography

● Use the internet to research information about the life and work of a well-known author. Make notes in the boxes below.

Introduction

Who is your biography about?

_____

_____

What are they best known for?

_____

_____

_____

Childhood

Where and when were they born?

_____

_____

_____

Where did they go to school?

_____

_____

_____

Family life

Are they married?

_____

Do they have any children?

_____

_____

What do they enjoy doing in their spare time?

_____

Career

What was the first book they wrote?

_____

Which book are they best known for?

_____

Have any of their books won awards?

_____

Illustrations © 2010, Mike Phillips/Beehive Illustration.

● Now write an author biography. Turn the notes in each box into a paragraph of writing with three or four sentences in it.

Section 2: Developing writing

Curriculum vitae

● Choose a historical figure, a fictional character or a celebrity and imagine you are that person. Think of a job that you would be well suited to. Create a CV including details of qualifications, experiences and interests relevant to the job you are applying for.

Name: _____

Position applied for: _____

Education/qualifications: _____

_____

_____

Employment history: _____

_____

_____

_____

Hobbies/interests: _____

_____

_____

_____

_____

Illustrations © 2010, Mike Phillips/Beehive Illustration.

writing guides

Medal winner

● Make notes under each heading as you listen to the audio clip of a medal winner being interviewed.

How she feels now.

_____

_____

_____

What she did before the race.

_____

_____

_____

How she motivates herself.

_____

_____

_____

Her plans for the future.

_____

_____

_____

Illustrations © 2010, Mike Phillips/Beehive Illustration.

News report

● Write a short newspaper report based on the information contained in the audio clip 'Medal winner'.

Writing guides

An evacuee's diary

● Imagine you have been evacuated from your home in the city. You will be staying with a family in the countryside.

● Complete the diary entry below.

I was sad to leave mum at the station this morning. I don't know when I will see her again...

Connectives

Connectives are words and phrases that are used to link clauses, sentences, paragraphs or chapters. There are four main types:

1. Time – used to indicate when something happened or to sequence ideas
2. Addition – used to add additional information
3. Cause – used to show cause and effect
4. Opposition – used to introduce a different point of view.

● Place these connectives into the correct column in the table.

first	because	also	but
therefore	consequently	some years later	
after	so	furthermore	however
finally	this means	before	additionally
	nevertheless	moreover	as well as

Time	Addition	Cause	Opposition

● Use a thesaurus to help you add more connectives to the table.

writing guides

Writing

Each of the writing projects outlined below requires the children to plan, write, edit and improve a biographical/autobiographical life story. The activities provide an opportunity for children to apply the writing skills they have developed when completing the activities in Sections 1 and 2.

- In Project 1, 'A real life story', children research, plan and write a biography for a particular person, such as a historical figure, or a grandparent. (Related activities include Section 1: Extract 3, 'Autobiography and biography'; Section 2: 'Life-story research', 'Timeline', 'Obituary', 'Author biography', 'Connectives'.)

- In Project 2, 'Life in the trenches', children plan and write a simulated autobiography of a modern-day soldier. (Related activities include Section 1: Extract 2, 'A memorable moment'; Section 2: 'This is my life', 'Writing for different audiences', 'Diary writing'.)

- In Project 3, 'The burglary', children plan and write an autobiographical/biographical account of an event, establishing and maintaining viewpoint in their chosen form of writing. (Related activities include Section 1: Extracts 1 and 2, 'Autobiography and biography'; Section 2: 'Writing for different audiences', 'Diary writing'.)

Using the writing projects

The teacher's notes provide step-by-step instructions on how to guide children through the writing process. Each writing project should be carried out over a number of sessions in order to allow children sufficient time to develop ideas, to plan and write a complete life-story text and to evaluate, edit and improve their work. All children should have access to a copy of photocopiable page 18 'Life stories poster' to remind them of the key features of the genre when planning and writing their own texts.

Using the writing templates

The four writing templates provided on the CD-ROM allow the children to produce their own life stories using images and text. Children can choose to produce their life story in the form of a biography, a letter, a diary or a report. They can type their life stories directly into one of the writing templates or the writing templates can be printed out for the children to fill in by hand. There is a selection of images available in the image bank that can be incorporated into the writing templates next to appropriate parts of the text. You will also need to show the children how to upload other images into the image bank by clicking on 'Our images' and 'Add' to navigate to where the image is stored. A thumbnail picture will be added to the 'My images' gallery.

Writing tips

- Select a form and writing style appropriate to the purpose and audience of the text.
- Write in the first or the third person.
- Organise information into paragraphs, sections or chapters with an appropriate opening and closing.
- Write in the past tense.
- Use a range of connectives to create links within and between sections.
- Include interesting detail about what happened to engage the reader.

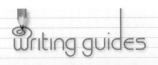

Project 1: A real life story

Objective

To experiment with the order of sections and paragraphs to achieve different effects.
(Year 5 Strand 10)

What's on the CD-ROM

Biography planner
- Use the template to make notes about the life of a particular person.

My life story
- Compose a biography using the writing templates.

What to do

In this activity, children research and write a biographical account of a particular person's life.

- Hand out photocopiable page 38 'Biography research'. Ask the children to choose a biographical subject, note down what they know about that person and think of some questions they would like to research.

- Provide opportunities for the children to research the life story of the person they have chosen. Ask them to make notes of key information on 'Biography planner' on the CD-ROM or photocopiable page 39.

- Hand out photocopiable page 27 'Timeline'. Ask the children to record significant events on and then organise the information into clear paragraphs for writing by dividing the timeline into several sections.

- Open writing template 'My life story: biography' on the CD-ROM. In shared writing, model how to expand one of the children's notes into a biographical life story.

- Ask the children to use the template to write a biographical account based on their research. Remind them to organise their writing into clear paragraphs and to use a range of connectives to link ideas.

Project 2: Life in the trenches

Objective

To establish, balance and maintain viewpoint in non-narrative texts.
(Year 6 Strand 9)

What's on the CD-ROM

Media resources
- Use the 'First World War trenches' photo to generate ideas for a piece of writing in role.

Hopes, fears and dreams
- Read the roll over text.
- Record ideas in the thought bubbles.

My life story
- Use the writing templates.

What to do

In this activity, children plan and write a simulated autobiography about a soldier on the front line.

- Look at the image 'First World War trenches' and discuss what the children already know about what life was like for soldiers in the First World War. Watch or read an extract from a film or text that describes conditions in the trenches, such as *Private Peaceful* by Michael Morpurgo.

- Use the drama techniques of freeze-framing and thought-tracking to explore what the soldier is thinking and how he is feeling. Use simple prompt questions to guide the children's responses.

- Hand out photocopiable page 40 'Life in the trenches' and ask pairs to note down descriptive words or phrases under each heading.

- Explain that you would like the children to draft and write a simulated autobiography based on the image, in the form of either a diary entry or a letter home to their family. Recall some of the characteristic features of these life-story texts.

- Ask the children to plan ideas using 'Hopes, fears and dreams' on the CD-ROM or photocopiable page 41; and to use their sheets to draft and write a life-story text in the form of a letter or diary entry. (Use 'My life story: a letter' or 'My life story: a diary' on the CD-ROM.)

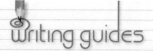

Project 3: The burglary

Objective

To set their own challenges to extend achievement and experience in writing. (Year 6 Strand 9)

What's on the CD-ROM

Media resources
- Use the 'Burglary' photo to generate ideas for a piece of biographical/ autobiographical writing in role.

The burglary
- Sequence the pictures.
- Complete speech bubbles.

My life story
- Compose a report, letter or diary entry using the writing templates.

What to do

In this activity, children plan and write a biographical/autobiographical account documenting a real life story.

- Display the image 'Burglary' from the CD-ROM and talk about what is happening. In small groups, ask the children to work in role using flashbacks and flash-forwards to explore what might have happened in the moments leading up to the burglary and immediately after the burglary. Encourage them to think of other people who may have been involved in the incident for example, a neighbour who phones the police or a police officer who apprehends the burglar. Take whole-class feedback of ideas.

- Open 'The burglary' activity from the CD-ROM and ask the class to sequence the pictures and complete the speech bubbles to show what some of the people are saying. Alternatively, children could complete the same activity using photocopiable page 42.

- Give out copies of photocopiable page 43 'The real story' and ask the children to make detailed notes about the incident from the point of view of one of the people involved. Allow the children to discuss and develop ideas with a partner.

- Explain that you would like the children to use the notes they have made to write a life-story text describing the incident. Ask them to choose an appropriate format for example, a letter, a private diary entry or a police report. They can then plan and draft a life-story text using writing template 'My life story: a letter', 'My life story: a diary' or 'My life story: a report' on the CD-ROM. Remind the children to consider the purpose and audience of their chosen form when deciding what, and how to write and encourage them to maintain a consistent viewpoint and style throughout.

- Share and evaluate some of the children's life-story texts.

Biography research

● Choose a person and use this sheet to start planning your biography.

I am going to write a biography of _____.

What I already know:

_____

_____

_____

_____

_____

_____

Questions I would like to be answered by
my research:

_____

_____

_____

_____

_____

_____

_____

_____

Illustrations © 2010, Mike Phillips/Beehive Illustration.

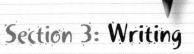
Biography planner

● Use this planning sheet to make notes about the life of a famous person of your choice.

Personal details
(Full name, date of birth, place of birth)

Background information
(Childhood, education and career, family life)

Important events
(Who? What? Where? When?)

Illustrations © 2010, Mike Phillips/Beehive Illustration.

Life in the trenches

- Imagine you are a soldier in the trenches. Make notes under each of these headings.

What can you hear?

How do you feel?

What can you see?

What can you smell?

Hopes, fears and dreams

● Imagine you are a soldier in the trenches. What are your...

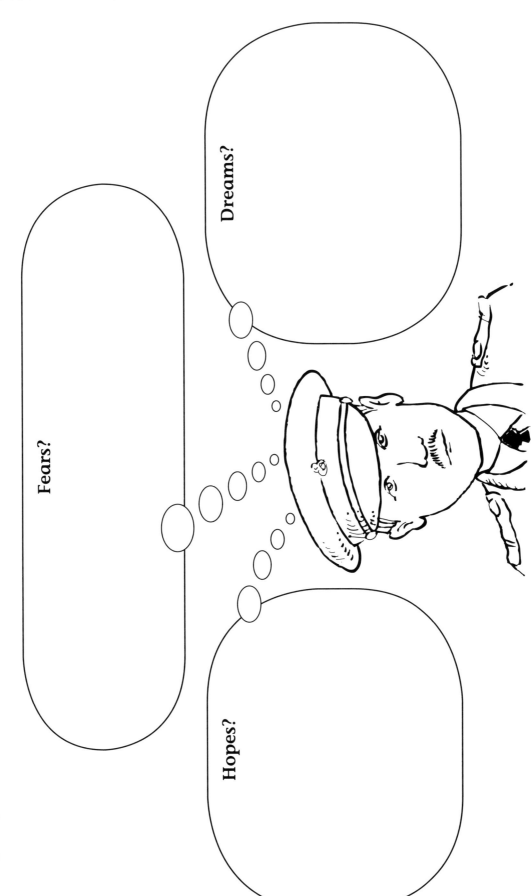

Dreams?

Fears?

Hopes?

Section 3: Writing

The burglary

● Number the pictures from 1 to 6 to show what happened. Fill in the speech bubbles to show what one person in each picture is saying.

Illustrations © 2010, Mike Phillips/Beehive Illustration.

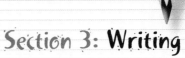
The real story

● Pretend that you are one of the people who were involved in the incident. Make notes about what happened.

Who are you?

_____

_____

Where and when did the burglary take place?

_____

_____

_____

Who was involved?

_____

_____

_____

What happened?

_____

_____

_____

How did you feel?

_____

_____

_____

How did the people around you react to the events?

_____

_____

_____

Illustrations © 2010, Mike Phillips/Beehive Illustration.

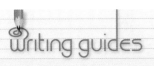

Section 4

Review

The review activities provide a framework for assessing children's understanding of and ability to use key features of life stories in their own writing. The activities on photocopiable pages 45 and 46, 'Self review' and 'I like that bit!', can be used by the children to review work in progress or to evaluate finished work. The teacher review sheet on photocopiable page 47 can be used to make an overall assessment of children's progress at the end of a unit of work.

Self review

Ask the children to review their written work against the success criteria contained in the checklist on photocopiable page 45. Provide opportunities for children to edit and improve their written work based on the outcome of the review.

Peer review

Photocopiable page 46 'I like that bit!' is for the children to use with writing partners or in small groups. Ask the children to read and review each other's writing by answering the questions. Ensure that the comments given are positive and supportive. The peer-review activity can also be used to help the children review their work in progress and produce an improved final version.

Teacher review

Carrying out an overall review of children's progress and attainment in writing at the end of a series of lessons on life stories will enable you to evaluate the progress individual children have made towards achieving specific learning goals. The outcome of the teacher review can be used to set group and individual learning targets and to ensure that the next steps in learning for all children are planned at an appropriate level. The review may also highlight gaps in the children's experiences. If this is the case, refer to the relevant activity in Section 2 to address these gaps.

The teacher review grid on photocopiable page 47 is modelled on the writing assessment guideline sheets produced by the DCSF and can be used to assess the children's work on life stories against national standards. The grid has been designed to enable you to record evidence of children's progress and attainment at the end of a series of lessons on writing life stories.

When reviewing a child's ability in relation to each Assessment Focus it is important to take into account a range of evidence including: Completed life stories – can the child write a simple biographical account organising writing into clear paragraphs or sections and using connectives to link ideas?; Planning and writing – Can the child use different sentence structures including complex sentences?; Speaking and listening – does the child use key structural and language features of life stories when recounting a life story orally to a partner?

Self review

● Read your story and tick the boxes if the statements are true.

Title _____

Text structure	I have written my life story in chronological order.	☐
	I have organised material into paragraphs/sections.	☐
	My life story has a clear opening…	☐
	…and closing.	☐
	I used connectives to link sentences.	☐
	I used connectives to link paragraphs/sections.	☐
Language features	I have written in the past tense.	☐
	I have used a mixture of simple, compound and complex sentences.	☐
	I have used interesting vocabulary appropriate to the purpose and audience.	☐
	I have written in an appropriate style.	☐
Sentence structure and punctuation	I have used full stops, question marks and exclamation marks to punctuate sentences.	☐
	I have used commas in lists.	☐
	I have used commas to mark clauses within complex sentences.	☐

I like that bit!

● Read your partner's life story. Tell your partner what you like about their piece of writing and how you think it could be improved.

I enjoyed reading this life story because _____

_____

_____

My favourite part was _____

_____

because _____

_____

The description of _____ (a person)

was great. It could be even better if _____

_____

The description of _____ (a place)

was really good. It could be even better if _____

_____

The most important event seemed to be _____

_____

It could be funnier/sadder/more interesting/exciting/scary if _____

_____

_____

I would have liked to know more about

_____

_____

_____

writing guides

Teacher review

Child's name: _____ Date: _____

	AF5 Vary sentences for clarity, purpose and effect.	AF6 Write with technical accuracy of syntax and punctuation in phrases, clauses and sentences.	AF3 Organise and present whole texts effectively, sequencing and structuring information, ideas and events.	AF4 Construct paragraphs and use cohesion within and between paragraphs.	AF1 Write imaginative, interesting and thoughtful texts.	AF2 Produce texts that are appropriate to the task, reader and purpose.	AF7 Select appropriate and effective vocabulary.
LEVEL 4	Some variation in sentence structure. *Use of some subordinating connectives, throughout the text.* (QCA Assessment guidelines for writing)	Uses full stops, capital letters, exclamation marks and question marks accurately to punctuate sentences. Commas used in lists.	Content is ordered chronologically or by grouping related points. There are clear opening and closing paragraphs.	Content is organised into appropriate paragraphs or sections. Simple connectives are used to link sentences. Evidence of attempt to use appropriate connectives to establish links between paragraphs/sections.	Content and ideas relevant to task. Adverbial and expanded noun phrases add detail. Appropriate viewpoint established and sustained.	Clear opening establishing the form and purpose of the writing. Purpose of writing may not be consistently maintained.	Uses vocabulary appropriate to task and audience. Some imaginative vocabulary choices used for effect.
LEVEL 5	Uses a range of simple, complex and compound sentence structures. *Wider range of connectives used to clarify relationship between ideas.* (QCA Assessment guidelines for writing)	A full range of punctuation used accurately and consistently across the text. Commas used to mark clauses within complex sentences.	Material is organised and developed in paragraphs/sections. The text has a clear ending that refers back to the opening.	Paragraphs are used effectively to structure ideas. A range of connectives is used within and between paragraphs to give cohesion to writing.	*Relevant ideas and material developed with some imaginative detail.* (QCA Assessment guidelines for writing) Appropriate writing style selected and used consistently throughout writing.	Writing shows clear awareness of purpose and audience. Purpose of writing consistently maintained. Uses and adapts features of life-story texts to suit audience and purpose.	Uses carefully selected vocabulary to create contexts and describe people, places and events.

![SCHOLASTIC]

Also available in this series:

ISBN 978-1407-11253-4

ISBN 978-1407-11265-7

ISBN 978-1407-11267-1

ISBN 978-1407-11256-5

ISBN 978-1407-11270-1

ISBN 978-1407-11248-0

ISBN 978-1407-11254-1

ISBN 978-1407-11266-4

ISBN 978-1407-11258-9

ISBN 978-1407-11268-8

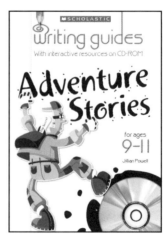

ISBN 978-1407-11251-0

ISBN 978-1407-11257-2

To find out more, call: **0845 603 9091**
or visit our website: **www.scholastic.co.uk**